# FROM THE NEANDERTHAL

BY THE SAME AUTHOR

POETRY

*Mornings in the Baltic*
*Meeting Montaigne*

FICTION

*Ulverton*
*Still*
*Pieces of Light*

# FROM THE NEANDERTHAL

Adam Thorpe

CAPE POETRY

Published by Jonathan Cape 1999

2 4 6 8 10 9 7 5 3 1

First published in Great Britain in 1999 by Jonathan Cape
Random House, 20 Vauxhall Bridge Road, London SW1V 2SA

Random House Australia (Pty) Limited
20 Alfred Street, Milsons Point, Sydney,
New South Wales 2061, Australia

Random House New Zealand Limited
18 Poland Road, Glenfield,
Auckland 10, New Zealand

Random House South Africa (Pty) Limited
Endulini, 5A Jubilee Road, Parktown 2193, South Africa

Random House UK Limited Reg. No. 954009

A CIP catalogue record for this book
is available from the British Library

ISBN 0 224 03971 7

MIX
Paper | Supporting
responsible forestry
FSC® C018179

Printed and bound in Great Britain by Clays Ltd, St Ives PLC
Typeset by Palimpsest Book Production Limited
Polmont, Stirlingshire

The Random House Group Limited supports The Forest Stewardship
Council (FSC®), the leading international forest certification organisation.
Our books carrying the FSC label are printed on FSC® certified paper.
FSC is the only forest certification scheme endorsed by the leading
environmental organisations, including Greenpeace. Our
paper procurement policy can be found at
www.randomhouse.co.uk/environment

*Every day things happen in the world that can't be explained by the laws we know about things. Every day they're spoken of and forgotten, and the same mystery that brought them takes them away, their secret converting into oblivion. Such is the law by which things that can't be explained must be forgotten. The visible world goes on as usual in the broad daylight. What's alien peeps at us from the shadows.*

Fernando Pessoa, *The Book of Disquietude*
(translated by Richard Zenith)

## ACKNOWLEDGEMENTS

Acknowledgements are due to the editors of the following: *Critical Quarterly, Hablar de Poesia, Independent, Jellyfish Cupful, London Review of Books, Poetry Review, Sibila.*

'Ghosts' was commissioned by the South Bank Centre.

# CONTENTS

| | |
|---|---|
| Against | 1 |
| Sketch | 2 |
| Tending the Stove | 3 |
| Errata | 6 |
| The Nine Ladies on Stanton Moor | 8 |
| Big Wheel | 9 |
| Rufus! | 10 |
| Twitchers | 11 |
| New Arrival | 12 |
| Fuck the Bypass | 15 |
| Wild Camping in Sweden | 16 |
| Ghosts | 18 |
| Pickings | 20 |
| Eva | 22 |
| Another Bad Year | 24 |
| King Cnut | 25 |
| Hot-Air Balloons from Marsh Benham | 26 |
| Fossil | 27 |
| Anniversary | 29 |
| Playground Accident | 31 |
| Lichen | 32 |
| Balkan Tune | 36 |
| Windows | 37 |
| Footprints | 40 |
| On the Beach | 41 |
| The Execution | 42 |
| The Exchange | 44 |
| Look | 46 |
| From the Neanderthal | 47 |

# AGAINST

*for Josh*

Against the bolts and welder's bloom of rhetoric
chamfer the waggon, scoop and shave the grain
to serviceable lightness, take the rein.

Against the packs of fighters shocking screes to fall
gaze on the heron, watch the wings wield their long
elegance over the water, echo the call.

Against the precipitate action of the angry father
loosen the mother, wait for the snow, hold
in a gloved finger his gloved hand, walk the lane.

# SKETCH

*for John Fuller*

I sketched my grandmother walking under the beech trees
where Grim's Dyke's little more than a hint of humps,
nettles in a shallow slump under a tangle of wire and posts.

Now she's gone. The sketch shows only a few lines of her,
but somehow it caught the way she walked in age,
and I do recall (I was nineteen) being amazed at the way it did.

The trees have not gone. The hint of humps, the suggestion
that here men constructed something bold and enormous for reasons
few are sure of, has not gone. The nettles are the inheritors

of the shallow slump of their forefathers my pencil suggested.
Everything is the same, one can say, except for the presence
of my grandmother, tiny in the picture, walking slowly away

and my amazed glance before I rose and called after her,
amazed that I could have caught her with a pencil's flicker –
knowing already that it would stay long after she was gone

as now she was gone into the beech trees' shade as if forever.

# TENDING THE STOVE

## NOVEMBER

The bole's on the block:
its fell already old, the bark puffs

at the first stroke of the saw
but the heart's harder: if time's

embodied anywhere
it's in this balking of a quick traverse –

each decade's felloe beaten only
by a lowered head, the chafe of now.

Sweaty, red-faced, I'll cut a day's worth,
a creamy pyramid of Os

with their exact configurations:
rolled-up maps the flames can scrabble at

or pore over, exultant
like us with our several plans.

## DECEMBER

We scour the river bank for flotsam,
poles the floods tore free of their leaves –

heroically long, dry from abandonment.
Criss-crossed, almost weaved, most caught

by a living trunk that rammed them
into stillness, we thought at first

they were nests – as if the wild boars
had bristled wings, had brought each bole

under massive, retroussé snouts, and fussed.
Yanked free and shouldered, our faggots

bounce behind us, shafts of chronology
so dense we feel a little queasy

as we reach the car. I've read
how most of the mornings of the world

are spent this way, but stumbled
ten miles for the twisted bough.

We lie, later, and talk by the heat
we feel we've earned in tart shoulders . . .

we glow. My life is a flicking of switches,
I think, as the lathering turbines roll.

JANUARY

Hours are devoted: the iron crown
perpetually up, ash snowing
the wrought name as I huff . . . *Godin.*

God in heat through a hard winter.
The knuckle-rapping flames would take
truck-loads, whole armies of timber

if we had it; toughs of holm oak,
brawny chestnuts scourged of sap,
the fizzling savagery of Hell

become the thrum of warmth we crouch to,
hands outspread. How millennial old
this altar, nurtured into embers

so high by evening we overheat . . .
like a late, imperial dynasty
dreaming in myth, it shuffles

4

its purple solely into ash, replete
with memories of the split carton's
ur-flame; the crackle of vine-butt; the sudden

resinous densities of laurel.

## FEBRUARY

As Basra is pounded to dust, I puff
old ash to glow
or tip the tray free, watching
the cloud it makes drift palely
into nothing, like history.

Abu Nawas, Hasan al-Basri –
old mystics fogeyish
as finger-bowls to the radio's
immediacies, old vowels
of the Abbasids, old blown-on ash

glowing in a man's eyes
short on humanity . . .
How fine this oyster-coloured
dust, this tossed smoke
floating importantly past the still trees.

# ERRATA

No sooner had we come
than already the misfeasances of history
recalled in the bullet-hole
some great-aunt could once locate
where the last priest to inhabit here
slumped, *un catholique*,

and the line high on the creepered mill
recording the flood
that took the miller's wife
and left him ruined, still
sued by the landlord
for lapse of rent.

I finger our stone wall, searching
as ever for resonance,
time's contusions, chips
off the old block. The washed-
up body of the miller's wife
is easy to imagine

now the rains have swollen
the river to a roar,
but the rest is harder: how
the harried widower fared, or what
purpose the shot priest served,
bundled by our step.

Now the times are quieter, rosy
with expectation, *le pittoresque*.
The shush of the D-road
mingles with the weir: each day
we speed past the cardboard plaque
on the dented roadside tree,

limply wreathed: IL AURAIT
EU 21 ANS
AUJOURD'HUI —
an execration increasingly faint,
a fact that each day makes
increasingly wrong.

We know you've got a thing about us,
scuffing the earth at our feet,
giving us a voice. Like this.

We know about the groans we've heard,
the yelps in moonlight, rumours of progeny.
Bellies keep pressing us; we decline.

Thunder on the moor and your effeteness
assured, we think of us as crown
whetted on the storm, not bald queans.

We know about the influx of coach parties;
the way their crisp-packet ordinariness
ruffles you, the way they laugh as they count us.

We have tumbled from the sky's favour.
We know we are emblazoned by tussocks,
heather, hawthorn. We have erred, somehow.

Stars! We look up to them. Clear nights
remind us of their massive dignities;
we know what we have known, but forgotten.

One of us is missing. We know this.
Buffed by the flanks of cows, she swings
a gate. We hear her, complaining, often.

Adrift on moorland, we are tethered.
Far off on a skyline, we have caught you.
We dance what we know; you are frozen.

Cromlechs rise routinely from mists:
we are granite lumps. We know
how ugly we are, and once how lovely.

# BIG WHEEL

I feinted with my vertigo and curved
to early middle age, I'd say; anyway
the top. There we were stopped and began to sway.
For my idiot daring it was all I deserved.

The remarkable vista of the environs of Gütersloh,
the backs of birds actually in flight, the shrubbery
of trees and the pinhead people made me rubbery
in the legs, of course, but what was worse was the slow

remorseless haul on my brain, or maybe my body
for the earth far below was wide and craving
my entry at whatever price. The kids were waving
and I started to wail, I'm afraid. I clung to the rod

and shut my eyes. You had to hold me tight.
In high air there was no bolt-hole from whatever
sirens were singing me down . . . as if I could sever
myself from this swaying life without a fight.

# RUFUS!

*for Emma*

Gloominess of oak and Tirel, gut-twanged treason
getting William – every passing forest's
running commentary for my sister's obsession.

*Rufus! Tell me about Rufus!* The Simca droned
and out it came again: from blundering boar
to wail of horn; the Fact that the King was alone.

*Thwack!* My sister in the back seat, covering her ears,
and me arched next to her, fisting my spine:
what makes most history something to be feared

is simply thwacks and *aaaaghs*, to a kid. I see us
speeding through the Sixties like a film,
the Simca's windscreen scrolling up the trees.

A legend gets it in the back from a dream.
History blunders into bracken to retrieve.
If I timed it right, I could make her scream.

# TWITCHERS

For every booming bittern there are ten,
for every cliff-stacked gannet mass

there is at least one with his clingfilmed
lunch-pack, wringing his socks on St Kilda.

This is surety of sorts. That the index finger
will go on twitching till the loch

gives up its greylag, the moor its merlin,
that even the chough has its hangers-on

grim-jawed on outcrops where the breakers sting
assures Him that all the aeons' messy fuss

holds some of them in thrall, despite the mockery.
When the Trumpets sound, drowning the guillemots,

when the souls rise like a billion fulmars
discarding behind them the stink of cerements,

when even the dotterel has shrilled its last
over the wrathful tussocks of Beinn Bhreac Mhor

He'll be there with his binoculars and notebook
spotting them: the Chosen, the ones who bothered,

the twits who noted His miraculous exactitude
all day in everything He could throw at them.

# NEW ARRIVAL

*for Miranda, much later*

The announcements mangle the names
of nineteenth-century villages:
Streatham, Norwood, Bermondsey.
The rest drowned in the vowels of the fast one to Brighton.

The platform indicator clicks to 6.
It's made by Solari and C. Udine,
Italy. Boredom yields such things,
presses them on you like a sales trick.

I think of Tarkovsky, the planet's brain
in *Solaris* like a broiling ocean.
They're sealing the roof in a fierce stink
of fibre-glass: there are so many jobs,

so many rules. We live in a world
of ladders and paint-splashed footstools.
Here it comes — always the one
with a friendlier look (if still aloof), the dummy

of the driver tiny in one of its eyes.
A schoolgirl drops her files, pushing
onto the carriage before me; her papers
wheel into a cogged underworld of grease.

The doors clam up, bad-tempered as ever;
pistol-shots to have us shake.
Humans make so much noise of the world.
It comforts us, I think. Death's to be deaf

and on one's own. Settled among litter,
I remember Cousin Ruth, my age;
at five, on a journey, she slapped some seats
like these, full of BR dust and something

strange that turned her blind and simple.
The guards are stranded for life between
thirty and fifty, sidle past
in cocked hats, condemned to being this cocky

or miserable, one with such long hair
his uniform is more an outfit.
Maybe they dreamt of being this,
as boys: whistling a real train into gear.

The platform removes itself discreetly
like a ship, along with its passengers,
or like a country with its population
staring as if curious, without compassion;

why does everyone look as though
they know what they are doing, as if
they have never *not* been here? The river
beyond the bolted trellis-work of bridge

is so wide we stop on it
for breath. The woman opposite
watches me read. My harmless book
becomes embarrassing, opening its legs of pages.

Her benign smile struggles against
the rapid blink of eyelids. Today
my wife's new niece had hers ungummed,
their two pale leaves now open to infection:

this is what life is. Duress
begins with the light, the looming faces.
We're really all too delicate for this,
this life, these jerks of some machine, this air.

At Charing Cross the metal turnstile
tries to keep.time with a cellist's Bach.
It doesn't, quite, and the effect is brutal.
Think of all the thighs its bar has pressed.

Toughen up. London yanks
us out and in like a clumsy midwife
and I make for the museums, the bookshops —
those cots where I can suck my thumb and dream.

# FUCK THE BYPASS

Cycling to the theatre on the 'other side',
I pass between the high wire fences
and feel the chicken. This is where the mammoth
project strides, like a pause in language,
a gasp between the murmurs of woods.

There are a thousand, ten thousand guards
in Pinkerton surcoats, helmets carnation-bright.
They laugh as I shout, scattered up the ridge
like a countermanded army, still confused.
Or flowers swelling where the ogre slew.

Each little lane demands a massive bridge
and likewise the winding Lambourn's stream –
where I tick now under a clear sky
will be thundered gloom too soon for this moment
to be more than dream, or a war's false lull.

The hedgerows return like cool pillows
discovered after nightmare, and I breathe again.
Yesterday's battle's caught its sleeve;
lying in the ditch before the old stone humpback
into Bagnor, the plastic hull of a duffed-up helmet's

scrawled all over in black felt-tip.
Curses that might or might not serve,
strangled war-cries, the head of the enemy
lopped and kicked and left to rot.
Keep it as souvenir of a strange time.

# WILD CAMPING IN SWEDEN

Our trouble at first was the pegs
our mallet got emphatically in
to the tufty pelt of needles;
they kept emerging. As if distrusted.

The lake bred plops of frogs
but we were alone on the bank.
A single boat nuzzled the crowfoot.
The whoop was when I saw the name –

I could hardly believe it. I told you
how I'd played him in the show –
the killing of Balder with the spear
of mistletoe (*him* on the sly)

and the hopeless ride to Hel
on Sleipnir, that refusal to cry
that made him much more evil
than trickster. Loki was a role

I'd very much enjoyed, distorting
my face to make the kids laugh
till the final enormity of malice
hissed me off (in tears). *Loki*'s

oars were in there, crossed like arms –
waiting demurely, it seemed. After
twilight we unlooped the chain
and sculled towards an island's hump.

The pines withdrew, the shore became a whim
below the huddled stars. That shriek
was a rowlock. We sped forward
as the prow chuckled and the hull

incited us with gleeful squeaks
to continue, despite the leaks.
No one roared from the shore
that we were thieves. The world was

as it was, before: a huge
unpeopled wood of pine and fir
with wealds of water for the moon
alone to look in. But you were still

so scared we had to turn back then.
Tying him up, I joked about Loki
the shape-changer, how the chain
had better be knotted fast

(what the gods had said, I said)
or he'd slip it with an otter's neck
and all night heard him scrape and slide
yards from the tent — surprised

to find him in the morning, snout
still nuzzling the crowfoot, firmly boat.
But the car wouldn't start. No reason.
And in all of mostly dead flat Sweden

we'd parked her at the bottom of a brief
but steep slope we couldn't get a grip on,
slipping and sliding its scree from under us
till I, for one, could have cried and cried.

# GHOSTS

*In memoriam. Camargue, 1995.*

What faces haunt us in our sleep
out of rolling combers
come from the deep; they are our dread

that there's not breath enough to save
the two whom we shall see
strolling over sand towards us, an age from death.

If they are limp in our arms and warm,
what wall now lies between us?
Was it the sea that delivered them so,

or have we blown too softly into their shells?
Let our lungs be taken with theirs
and stretched as trophies on the shelves of Tartarus;

amidst the kite-clattering winds
that they dragged for the elusive, silvery thing
there was air in plenty for our shouts

(as the firm heads rolled in our hands)
of despair. Let the two go well
into their separate sands;

keep about their necks their good-luck chains
and do not clothe their nakedness.
If what slipped on their flesh was our hands

scrabbling for the heart's impatience,
its pluck, pounding our palms upon a drum
that did not sound, then do not blame us

who hold the taste of their death in our mouths,
whose skin is tainted by their failing.
They'll come to Tartarus with the bruises

we planted: how they came by these wounds
is living's business, not to do with there —
that life can be left so easily under a flail of blows

sufficient to strike death cold
and bring the aghast blood back to its senses
makes us wonder why the waters

should ever have delivered us
from the gilled and ghostless world
into this, induced by breath

and the profit of a certain dryness.
Limp amphibians, those who are drowned
are guests among the anchors and the amphorae;

like the other dead, they do not rest for long,
dwelling in our dreams or the gull's mute song.
(Or are in hiding, and have not truly gone.)

# PICKINGS

Our ogres' steps of earth,
dug, yield a trove

of what they used to chuck:
keys stuck in rust's lock,

lots of bits of pot,
jabs in glass for goats

and knobs for doors long shut
from hands; each clink is luck

or a stab of sharp loss.
Jaws laid as if meant,

hips like open wings,
the lead weight of a wine

glass, snapped at the neck.
Tins, the tines of forks,

light francs from the war,
each worth what we find

to say about it; words
strung back to phrase a dream

lost like the old dame
who lived here when *le maire*

was a boy (who'd see her
propped in the dark door

with a bowl of gruel, a grin),
laid to rest just where

we light up all these things.
'She's much too deep,' I say –

my kids in hope she'll rise
one day, tucked on a spade,

like the small flask I earthed
once but did not break

marked *Prix 3 Frs,*
*'La Miraculeuse'.*

# EVA

*for our children*

She outwitted history.
Now the memory of her runs in your blood.
You have a great-grandmother
who outwitted it, and may her
jinking ability course in you
when the guns come and you need it.

You might, you might! She, once,
was a pretty little thing —
Warsaw, timber-yards, the future as sweet.
Between that garden and us
they trundled the unimaginable
guns you couldn't crouch from.

Cousins — she had so many cousins!
The unimaginable took them, and now
they are stranded in their frocks
in albums: pretty little things
for always. And her sister.
And her sister's son.

She jinked while the others
stayed put, or ran too straight.
Her pride, her anger: *Germans, Poles —
all pigs!* Forget and forgive
in that order, that was the problem.
The tea trembling in its saucer.

She jinked to the end, in the ward:
that last, intent stare above the mask
and the sudden grip that made me lean
to whatever she was telling me,
in silence. The writer's hand.
That grip on it. Everything else

slipped, slipping away at last.

# ANOTHER BAD YEAR

Each time we look for definitions
the river rubs the bank away.
No one can say
where the edge is with any precision

for the floods come most years
flailing their detritus of trees,
the hawthorn seized
in the teeth of the surge, sheared

rock whetted on the pelted mountains.
Here was a kink scythed through
to a reach, a new
and ruthless look that'd cuff our shins

were we to stand where we did
a week ago: and here our boots stay dry
where the swirl once tried
to shock us, where our bare heels slid.

Look, a broken chain marks the mooring —
here nothing's held sacred
or for long: the acres
splash where the barley swung, the floor

hits the ceiling and a family flees
or can't and stops. But the rain has no routine
and doesn't mean
to heft us under, to leave us in trees.

# KING CNUT

Cnut, knotted against it, toggled and bound
like a furrier's bale on the wharf,
marmenill from the knees down, taking it ill,
loathes the blatant ocean and possibly spits
though the wind returns it to its owner.

Knowing that this'll mark the annals forever –
spritelier than battles lost and won, outbreeding
his sons and the sons of sons, clotted
and burred on the long cloak of repute –
he stands and does not turn, but hums

with the surf outwrestling his shins
something a child might hum to encourage sleep.
The people, cudgelled from the cliff's summit,
merge into gulls. Cnut would like to interrogate
the sky or sail for weeks to the other edge

and shields his eyes with his hand an inch
under the crown's unrivalled metalwork.
Either the sky contends with the swell out there
or commands it. It is relatively simple.
Only the land succumbs, lets its pebbles sink like kings.

# HOT-AIR BALLOONS FROM MARSH BENHAM

None of them fret.
They bloom from the inaccessible parts of trees,
creak past our roofs

then roar
with, for God's sake, a tongue of flame
under the hemmed-in air.

Insouciant:
exactly what they make you feel you aren't
as the fields yield them

from where you thought
you'd be panting towards for their lives
through lustrous moths of smut.

# FOSSIL

*Nürnberg, 1997*
*for Sabine Hagenauer*

The first globe was modelled here,
in Dürer's time;

now we climb the steps of Hitler's stadium,
tight-lipped, secretly aghast.

This is where he flipped
and the world followed, spun

by so many leather gloves
it took this pleasant park to hold them.

A playpen for demons,
their beaten childhoods, it's fanged

by broken glass and twisted cans.
It seems too vast to be bombed,

or delivered from its past.
These are not steps, but seats;

the Romans sat on theirs
for long enough to wear out dips

but Nazi bottoms barely polished these.
Then I spot, puffing near the top,

a small shell whorled into the stone
like a birthmark,

a sort of saving scar;
what years it swam to end up here,

numbered in the lives this arena took,
whose wall-eyed thrash was never dignified

by such seniority of time but mocked,
mocks also all that loss.

# ANNIVERSARY

*for Jo*

Butterflies iced on the wedding cake
as if my own had flown and settled there;
Mike with his home-made reflector out of card
behind him like a strange bloom, looming up
on so many feasting
who have since departed the warmth for good.

His photos show us how we stood,
not how full of winter air the cheeks were
when we kissed them, nor how fast the blood
came back like luck in the wood-lined, tin-walled hut
that day of sheer
steady joy in a polar poise of fields.

Time's wedded to what it wields,
shirks nothing after the day; we do not know
as the happy couple or as sozzled guest
how touch and go this is, nor what misgivings
might give way to:
boredom smoulders but may not ever catch.

The crossed threshold, the dropped latch;
like a furious mist the future veils its shapes,
but not today. The past is given away
with the bride, the present toasts itself with pride
and cannot say
more than something it will not regret.

Happiness is caught with its mouth still wet,
looking shyly at us from the mirror, twelve
years on; what we really meant that day
still means, and the candid criterion of children
holds us in thrall
to their love, their here-bound and tearful being.

With glass in hand, each moment fleeing
our gaze, we'll again not mind the empty restaurant –
the first hard frost falling as it always does
this November night; remembering the mothball vestry,
the stroke of the pen
that signed us to this forever in the parish

register of 1820: our marriage
drying on the page there only to stay
among shepherds, spinsters, clerks and milkmaids,
binders, thrashers, all the vanished trades
and teachers like us –
right back to the first, that awkward cross,

its butterfly kiss long flown from loss
not cited here but through the vestry's door,
outside, where some names share a page again
of stone this time, and mossed, and hard to read.
So to the death,
my love: as it was said, and as I still believe.

# PLAYGROUND ACCIDENT

My son's forehead's snickered across
yet again by thread; like tiny flies
the stitches have settled for days, but a year
and a half is the scar's reign,
according to the doctor.

All his life remains
to bounce off where it's hard enough
(this time a gate) for boys of eight
to bloody themselves, for grown men to wail.
Where the font-shell's sacred water

made him cry that day in church,
I press the lint. He's brave, now.
I remember the stain his birth made
on the carpet, its rose preserved
long after his head had been washed

of the perfumed afterbirth
that streaked it. He admires his wound
in the mirror: walking back from school
this evening, he was feinting (I saw)
with a rapier cast from air

and God knows where he was, then.
I think of war and all that wars
have done so far to our families' pasts –
his hurt is his, not mine,
but what I bear less well

than dabbing at the flesh of my flesh
lightly split by iron
is the thought of the unknown
iron that remains:
of all this head must pass.

# LICHEN

Winster's rocks my father clambered over
welcomed you and I each morning
from the cottage window, back of Main Street.

Laval lumps like a giant's porridge
left out all night, flanked by oaks
yet gaunt and still on the skyline.

I'd lean on the sill and stare it
into my father's boyhood, immensely
long ago but close enough to touch,

and he in turn imagining his mother's –
and she her mother's in a strange skirt,
clambering the clefts and ledges to the 'summit'.

This is my pedigree. I cling to it.
I cling to the place where the lava cooled
for as good as forever and the clump's

endurance was surer than sunlight
for God knows how many souls in this stony dale,
measured by whatever weather brought them

to the coffin. Trees come down or grow
but rocks don't. Neither does a skyline offer
more than the changing of light or the rim

of what is loved or hated. Nor do the houses
mean more than what is scrabbled for within –
the faces that alter as the sky does, and the barren fields.

Only the rocks were the hub, I think,
the nave through the turning wheel;
those ugly, lovely lumps I'll one day

bring my own to (the cottage sold)
and let them clamber; and tell them how,
once, on a visit, I did the same

in schoolboy shorts and odd haircut
while my father told how he'd done likewise
day after day till the war came.

So flimsier it grows, the chain;
prehistories of hand-holds and lost squeals,
my father's boyhood careering down the slope

in a race only the rocks reveal
the outcome of, bare against the twilight:
landmark of lives and lava,

bearer of tiny fonts in the wet,
gathering acorns in the folds
of its rough skirt between the fairy flax

and sea-complexioned assimilations
impressed on it in furry crusts
neither quite living nor dead

the clumsiest boot won't mark
but softer to the grasp than where it's not.
Softer, and with a million delicacies

of coarseness, of points and frills
and microscopic continents of mouths
sucking in the clean air's wet,

the pelt of the lichen remains
rootless as paint on the outcrop,
on the bumps and ledges, in the clefts.

It grows so slowly, but it grows
and dies out under itself, carbuncles
to a bristly grey or ripples to a stain

or crawls its moss over itself once more
so rock just there looks as if it's breathed
and has a mind, has awareness.

For lichen is more the phantom of the rock
than the desire of the rock to be covered
in fur, to rise as a living thing;

so barely clinging to the world
we know from the leaves, from the stem
that shoulders out of mud, it seems

of another order, of the order of memory –
of the like fragility and farness
as my father careering down the slope

on an evening of his boyhood
as his mother runs up in an earlier year
and another century, passing through him

to the place he's come from and clambering there
as I did once, on a visit. And so thereafter
(when I was old enough to liken

lichen to memory), approaching
with a slower tread and the fear
that I would never really know

this place as they once did, nor lay
my ghost upon more than paper,
make no more headway than the last

hand-hold, no more impression
than this brief rearing on the lean
ridge of the keystone boulder

with its view through the oaks
of the field's skyline and the ruined barn . . .
The rootless lichen marauds

inch by inch through the years,
prey only to pollution – like lemon
squeezed on an oyster's frill

our air tests it until it dies.
I cannot remember what has changed
or whether its pattern has remained

to tease me into seeing faces
that were always there, or feel
under palms the reassuring fur

at the same heave. While the rocks
wear so well we can be sure
heirs as far from us as stars

will look upon the same
under an ageing sun
(the closest we will come to eternity),

at least there is something to guess
about lichen; whether it was,
whether it might not be there.

# BALKAN TUNE

She knew a massive heap of songs,
her lullabies were ancient wrongs.
The mad were coming to their senses.
Beat the washing. Repair the fences.

Twilight came when sheep cropped faster
in her sullen neighbour's pasture
to one now blind; and she would see
her father lying like a tree,

the flock like stones, the plane a speck
and she again too small to check
the blood that sped where he'd been strafed:
the shepherd who had stood and waved.

But what did *she* do to be killed?
For here she lies where she's been spilled
by drunks in combat gear for wrongs
trickling from her throat like songs.

# WINDOWS

In every job I did
there was always a soldier, ex-
but still short-haired, and trembling

with a great violence.
Up at the truck-yard, for instance,
where I was re-puttying the windows

he'd stride across
from the body shop and shout at me
*Gerron you fucker* as I was wet-

thumbing the paste on;
I'd grin aimlessly, loosening the flakes of paint
from mouth and eyebrows as he

slammed the pressure-hose
to clean a juggernaut, water howling
at the hub-caps, riddling the grille.

Later on, when I had
reached the paint stage, carefully sweeping
leagues of deep blue on the frames I'd filled

of the yard's windows, he'd
come right over on one of those errands
that involve a lot of clanking

in a bag of tools,
and after the usual *Lookin at me fucker?*
or *Wot's the game then, la-di-da?*

or *You couldn't paint
to save your fuckin balls*, he
softened, slowly, and when I asked him

(running my brush along
the hardened putty at the pane's cliff-edge)
where he'd been in the Army

he paused, then stopped what-
ever he was doing and stood by the ladder
and he talked. I'm not quite sure

whether to believe him
on reflection, but then and there,
as the winter darkened in the glass

towards the day's end, and desperate
engines were revved in the distance
and the stink of diesel drifted like fog,

he nodded at what he said: *Three
fuckin years in Northern Ireland, sleepin
in the backs of fuckin trucks . . .*

*Let me tell yer, when
it's said that a Paddy's fuckin blowed
hisself up, it's lies*

*more 'n likely: you know
what they do? Fuckin saw it, too.
We found one bastard with his Ford Cortina*

*stuffed full. I watched it as they
booted him black, then cut off his tool. Tied him
to the gelly in the back of the motor*

*and ran for fuckin cover.*
*Arms 'n' legs blown high as the sky, along with the tool.*
*Don't leave no fuckin evidence, see.*

An engine chugged beyond
the gaffer's shed. The sign said *R. E. Bates* – who liked
to join us in the tea-break, talking horses,

the progress of his vegetables,
while I'd plough through my Patrick White. The ex-regular
stared at my brush as I eased its load

along the critical line.
I tutted, amazed, and said I found it incredible,
the blue welling up too thick

at the corner, too full
on the brush, nowhere to go but the glass
of the machine shop, smeared. He left me

to my clumsiness, my dread
that Old Man Bates would find me like this, mopping up
as best I could: it was his yard.

In a few years' time
every blue-eyed shop and shed I'd done
with such skills as care alone could muster

would be bulldozed, after the site was sold.

# FOOTPRINTS

*for Sacha*

We're walking over the highest hills of France,
my son on my shoulders, and he's on to footprints now,
the prints of boots and dogs in the path's slough
between the stunted pines and heather and flung grass.

He wants to know where ours are. 'Ours are behind.'
'Why aren't our footprints there in front?' 'Because
we're not there yet. Footprints come out from us.'
'Footprints aren't ever where you haven't been'd?'

'No.' My wife carries our seven-week-old daughter
in a sling. He wants to see his sister make some.
'She's much too young.' 'She'll make them soon!' 'You're aching
my shoulders – make some now instead of later.'

He says 'Oh yes' and I let him down. He runs
ahead, then turns and looks. Beyond is already
what has and has not been: the light fading,
the wind that over the hill-tops sweeps this rain.

# ON THE BEACH

The sun is warm, October slants
across molten cobalt's hiss and sheen,
gilding the knuckles of foam around the knees

of my children: what are our gods, in the end, but these
few moments in a life when we're at ease
with it all, conscious that we're being taken for a ride

but helpless to mind between the bull's horns?

# THE EXECUTION

*What was I to look for in this land of persecution and reprisal . . . ?*
R.L. Stevenson, *Travels with a Donkey in the Cévennes*

No doubt he'd walk it in stout shoes, two minutes
to muster thought and clear his throat, pause
perhaps to admire God's handiwork of vines
then enter and fiddle with the candles as always

in a sober dark, in those constant vestry odours
shared with the tallest cathedrals of the North . . .
mouldy cloth, the cluttered simulacra
of God's presence collecting dust. No doubt

he'd have listened to the river still chuckling past
to the far weir's hiss and groped for some metaphor –
perhaps the mill-wheel's drench downstream, that flood.
A poorish man, he'd have found some consolation

in the loveliness of place, would have heard
the first boots scrape the slabs between
peasant mutters with more love than rancour.
So, no doubt, when the Camisards came, this good

Catholic was brave: yanked from his wine,
shoved against the wall, all he's bequeathed
us is a flurry of nicks to be fingered for
long after the flintlocks cleared from their puffs

(a thing he never saw), along with the loathing
that steadied them. Yet, putting our door to
and taking, as he did, the same two minutes
to gaze on cirrus past a roof of ilex

bursting out of walls in a place now common
(the rain only hallowing the mysteries of briar
I high-step through to where the altar stood),
it's doubtless too easy to assume the worst,

the nave shrilled like this with cicada
and the river chuckling as it chuckled then:
that none of this missed him, or could even grace
what case-shot made of him, blurring our wall.

# THE EXCHANGE

*(Durchausen, Germany)*

We pass a wayside crucifix and Anna
(four and a half) asks, 'Why that man, he fall
in the water?' 'Which man?' 'That man.'

She's pointing at the rood. I'm tempted to pass.
I look for water, see only withered flowers
but yards off as we are there might well be

a basin, closer. This intrigues me. 'Jesus,'
I say, 'that's Jesus. There isn't any water.'
She's brewing up a storm: 'Why – he –

fall – *in?*' The tortoise slowness of adults. We go
over; the jar of blooms is wilted, there is
no water. Jesus hangs in copper, unpainted

on a cream cross beneath the apple's boughs
laden with fruit. I say again there is no water.
She stamps her foot and tries a different tack:

'Well *why* they hung him up to *dry*, then?'
My collapse into laughter annoys her, and so I find
I'm suddenly describing the nails, the pain,

what it was all supposed to be for. She looks
at the dappled ground, the cows in the field, and then
at Him, still as bedraggled. She doesn't say

a word. I've changed the pegs to nails, and frankly
I'd prefer her version any day.
Walking to the recreation ground, she keeps

her silence. It is as if she's letting it in —
the knowledge of this odd world where men do do
such things then put them on display, like teddies

dangling from washing-lines, not smelling nice
but hung to make them sad. Meanwhile I'm giggling
within, rinsed clean, the world made mad in the right way.

# LOOK

Only the eye's lens does not age. Old as us,
it holds out gamely, gazing into time
as the rest remakes around it: skin,
nails, hair – every cell of their grounding,

every glistening hidden interior thing
repairing itself, rewiring to newness,
suckling on the protein of its own thrust
so nothing remains as it was for long

except the lens, the gaze of the iris,
the least impermanent thing about us,
subduing only to senescence
in the milky cataracts of my mother

the lasers seared from her, etch by etch,
delicately scouring the one part of her
unchanged from the womb, the diamond
hardness of the softest bit – the glance

of the newborn, the child, the lover;
the calm pool stormed by tears, the blusters
of growing; by those gritty mornings after bombs
when history hung to be blinked at,

the harmattan, the chlorine of the deep ends;
the salve of distress, grief's soft curtain
over the unbearable sights, the old sufferings
or the squeezed lemons of laughter;

and I think how fitting it is that the rest
falls away, endlessly remade, while a glance
remains immaculate – Donne's windows
of the soul, that gazed on the womb's red light,

admitting the permanence of unplumbed depths
others dive into, or query with leads,
shafted otherwise only by a life's daylight
or the serious dreams of the eyelid.

# FROM THE NEANDERTHAL

1

In the blank spaces between words
a bird flies. I would like a marsh
where cranes alight in the way cranes do

and geese chase the dead
all the way to wherever
for my landscape this afternoon:

no people have yet been born this year.
This year, there is something to be said
for the way that curious, now extinct bird

has the sky to itself for a second.


2

Aspens thrill in the spring wind.
Our roots go down
ridiculously far

for the time of year.
For the time of year
is the aspen's,

and even a boy
on his thirtieth month
may bend an aspen

hand over hand, not very high up.

3

Our bundles have a weight, as if
there is something about God in them,
about clouds that hover as clouds do not,

about shoulders and clouds and God.
We pant to the brim in our lungs
where all sorts of boundaries begin.

We stop. We undo our bundles and cast
clouds of our own on the boulders
with the odd tiny bone like a vole's femur

and something that might have been well, once.

4

One day, we took a boat
and the reeds welcomed us.
Geese were hoarse but we ducked

and where the darkness started
we decided to cease
all quarrels with the sky

and sleep. Mammoths roamed
in our dreams, contented
with their lot. When we awoke

what absence of tusks crowded round us!

5

Where the high-rise gives way
to our time-span at last
one of us was slain in a wood:


woods are not where we like to call
so we left his death to itself
and made for the air. He was slain


where the wood's ferns are large
and the sunlight courts their spores.
We don't know where he was slain, really.


I made it up on the hoof. Woods are like that.


6


There was, indeed, an immense wrong done.
The punishment was punishment enough:
exile till death, a haircut to shrink from.


I saw him running along the crag one day,
and called: a big white sky
hanging by its talons from the very limit.


He shouldn't have been running
at a time like that. He must have forgotten
the whole machinery of the seasons


as I'd forgotten him, or the wrong.

7

If I could bear our shaft of ash on my shoulders
and return the core flint to its former
unfashioned self, things might look up

for all of us, since the catastrophe.
The wind is making play with our children,
the basic premise has slipped some mooring

and we aren't as far advanced as our ghosts.
We need to move and return to the origin.
The rumbles are the vying of our stomachs.

If I could grow a flower, it would be something.


8

Keeping pace with the snow like this,
we move so fast we might meet yours one day.
Imagine that, as the seers do, cupping their moths

or pointing to the city where the grass waves
a long farewell between this one and the next.
The next will come on the back of a grub.

It will pretend to be a fir for a while.
Among the uncountable forests of fir
there is always the one with a grudge against us,

biding its time between the snow and the snow.

9

Supposing, one of us said ten years before
where we are now, with a worrying moon,
one of us was bald all over the face

like the ghost we saw that day, in daylight.
The funerary rites: there is something anxious
about the sheer quantity of petals

we throw upon the smell. I hope
the change of climate will be taken by us all
one day at a time. There is nothing more

irritating than fashioning a drift.


10

The industry of flint work guides me back.
This morning I needed to study the plover
for my baccalaureate in things and how.

It rained soon after, deciding to be sleet.
I returned with the news that in fact
the plover's no plunger; that its cry

belongs; that the sliding grassland below
is not necessarily in pursuit.
The plover I described is not the other plover,

though the ultimate effect is the same.

11

In all uses of the term 'modern',
we are always available. Our hearth is as long
as my arm. Our smoke definitely longer.

Up, down, down, up. Horizontally speaking,
the infinite depends on our feet.
There is nothing we could do that we cannot.

Only the tiger appals us more
than our own intelligence. Even the thought
of its big pelt shaking off snow

might bring one leaping through a clever brow.

12

There are various matters to be seen to,
but I need the landscape to swallow
more than procreational activity

this afternoon, so I drift to the boulder.
Great danger attends the lone one, as once I
will be old. Anyway, here is the view.

Tundra. White birch holding purple thickets
either before or after. Whin, too.
Right now it's in a crucial phase of sheer

lichen. When I stand up, the sky does too!

The fuss attending the corpse is birds.
Meat is everyone's prerogative.
We're hauling on tendons with our teeth

at least twice since, plus the singe of moss.
Your lights bother me at times, in my sleep.
They criss-cross and spear and dazzle

as up they growl or grind like bears
the crag of my nightmares. Our refuge must be
plumb in the way, just as over the grasslands

clouds make their shadows move swifter than them.

In the upside-down bit of the lake
the plovers are just as good at swimming
as their aerial partners: they imitate

so exactly I have the heretical thought
that they might be the same, that a being
can occupy two places without splitting

and roar to scare the weakness away.
My partner, struggling with a duck, looks up
and hisses. I have brought, of course, a now

extinct *genus* of wolf the width of my fear.

From the moment she invented the cradle, perhaps.
Where our vague recognition, *advance*,
took shape and wing, fluttering in our heads.

Our heads became cages before the cage was invented.
Now we think in these flocks of geese and starling.
Some with the arrow-heads of geese.

Some with the twirling scarves of starling.
I think the geese are a head ahead, frankly,
barking the ghosts to their slumbers.

The noise these thoughts make affronts, but they pass.

The wind hauls the dawn into our home
for the night, making us leave it
for fear of ceasing on the spot. The boulders

here bear smiles of lichen: inviting types
between whose tufts of emergent firs
all manner of cracks might open up

into chasms: we keep to the tops, leaping
like goats, the type with curious hind legs
that swiftly dissolved through the following epoch,

the one that was merciless with oddities.

In the period of the juniper berry's ripeness
and the blue bilberry, we confronted a fire.
A high bluff of air had decided to flame.

It flamed and walked. Pine trees toppled
towards us. It flamed and walked quite steadily on
through the bilberry fields and the ripe juniper.

The sky took it as its lover. The procreational
activity of wind and flame was a wonder
that singed our foreheads and brought us the pain

continuance entails and which death runs from.

The seer said here will be traffic. Where the pipeline
runs unattended, legends of Yetis. The rocks will smile
and many people will tumble in a heap. Big ideas

will replace the long-toothed tiger in nightmares
and many the mammoth never born, herds and herds of them:
like a great inconvenience to the earth

bravely borne, the great pelts trailing juniper branches
and literally quivering at each percussion
of ice on hoof not equipped for something

he can't quite see, but is longer than an afternoon.

The shrubs are gathering in
their signs and symbols:
it is winter again.

So frail, the summer,
I would like to plait it
like grass, and keep my place

in the book of my life
forever, now, here.
I've noticed this is not possible.

Something is always ushering us.